INTRODUCTION

In the olden days hardly anyone reached the age of 50. The reasons for this are unknown and are still being studied by archeologists. But, in modern times, many young fellows reach their 50th birthday while feeling and sometimes looking much younger. Since few brave souls can picture themselves "HALF A CENTURY" old, this book will give people suspicious of nearing this mark a few tips on how to identify themselves.

Women, of course, never ever reach the age of 50 and this book is not at all for them. The oldest woman known to exist is in her 40's and this phenomenon is adequately covered in our last book "I'd Rather Be 40 Than Pregnant."

You add "GOD WILLING" to the end of most of your statements.

You know you're over 50 when

You are absolutely positive they build stairs steeper these days.

Someone calls you "POPS." (Sometimes someone calls you "CHIEF," or even a seemingly middle-aged gent calls you "SIR" or "MISTER.")

You know you're over 50 when

You keep forgetting. No matter how many diaries, appointment books, or calendars you have, you still forget. You write notes on slips of paper and then forget where you put the slips. Sometimes you call your kids by the wrong names.

All the money you saved for years for your children's college education just about covers the first semester.

You know you're over 50 when

You're asked to act as umpire or ref much more often than to participate on teams. You get tired just wrestling with your conscience.

Your arms aren't long enough to hold your reading material.

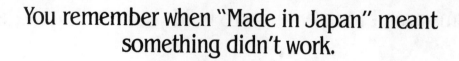

You remember when "Made in Japan" meant something didn't work.

You don't care where your wife goes when she goes out, as long as you don't have to go with her.

Getting a little action means your prune juice is working.

You start believing the ads for hemorrhoid, constipation, and hair loss remedies.

You still think of "grass" as something you cut.
You remember when smoking cigarettes was fashionable.

You know you're over 50 when

Attractive women at the office feel safe enough to flirt outrageously with you.

You start to hang around with new grandparents. Of course, most of them are much older than you are.

Watching sports on T.V. seems to be a much more sensible pastime than risking tearing yourself apart by playing the sports yourself.

Your music isn't their music.

Your kids are making more money than you. ("Johnny's daddy" has been changed to "the Doctor's father.")

You know you're over 50 when

No matter how many push-ups and sit-ups you do, and no matter how far you run, you finally resign yourself to no longer being a "HUNK."

You know you're over 50 when

You feel like the "morning after" and you can swear you haven't been anywhere.

You know you're over 50 when

You sit down to put on your underwear. The younger guys in the locker rooms have colored shorts but yours are all white.

You'd rather eat ice cream than frozen yogurt. You're not so sure about yogurt in any form unless your family is from the Middle East.

You think "Software" is a new comfortable undergarment and "Time-Sharing" a kind of romantic togetherness.

You give up trying to learn the names of all those African countries. At least you could spell the Belgian Congo and Rhodesia.

You think GAY means jolly, cheerful, and vivacious.

Picking up the balls seems to be almost as much work as it used to be playing the game.

You choose your cars for comfort and productivity rather than sex appeal, unless you are single again in which case you opt for total outrageousness.

Instead of combing your hair you start arranging it.
There is more hair on your chest than on your head.

You know you're over 50 when

The sports you do participate in require the use of braces, bandages, and protective gear that draw pitying glances from spectators.

Your back hurts. You see doctors, osteopaths, chiropractors, and therapists; you change your mattress, buy special shoes, wear braces, do exercises, take pills, and hang upside down, and it still hurts.

People keep saying "You haven't changed." This is the culmination of the 3 stages of life: youth, middle age, and
YOU HAVEN'T CHANGED.

People you used to hold in awe like doctors, policemen, and clergymen start being younger than you.

You know you're over 50 when

You start dressing for comfort rather than blindly following the latest fashions. Your color coordination takes a back seat to expediency.

You are finally smart enough to hire a kid to mow your lawn.

You wear vests to hide your stomach rather than to be with the latest fashion.

You may still be in the "rat race" but you no longer feel you have to win it.

You know you're over 50 when

You don't always wake up "aroused" like you used to every day.

You eat less and less and yet you still continue to gain weight.

You know you're over 50 when

You are vaguely suspicious of "new" foods such as sprouts, tofu, sushi, and seeds.

Your kid's motorbike costs more than your 1949 DeSoto did.

You have hats in your closet but never wear them anymore. You don't throw them out because you can never know when they might come back in style.

You know you're over 50 when

Growing melons brings you almost as much satisfaction as fondling them once did. You remember when "boobs" referred to dumb kids.

When people talk about drugs you think of penicillin. You don't quite understand all the controversy over "coke."

55 MPH seems a very reasonable and safe speed to travel at.

You know you're over 50 when

All the things you threw out the last time you moved now seem to be "Collectors items", and worth a fortune.

You really have to concentrate to call "Girls", "Women". You remember when calling "Women" "Girls" was a compliment. Your not quite sure if you're allowed to call them "Ladies."

IVORY TOWER PUBLISHING COMPANY INCORPORATED

These other fun books are available at many fine stores or by sending $3.50 ea. directly to the publisher.

2000 - Do Diapers Give You Leprosy? A humorous look at what every parent should know about bringing up babies.
2008 - Adult Connect The Dots. You played connect the dots as a child, but never like this!
2015 - Games You Can Play With Your Pussy. And lots of other stuff cat owners should know.
2020 - A Coloring Book for Pregnant Mothers To Be. Tender and funny, from being unable to see the scale to controlling your proud parents.
2026 - Games You Can Play In Bed. A humorous compendium covering everything from Bedtime Bingo to Things To Do at 3:45 A.M.
2027 - How To Pick Up Girls. Bridget is back to show all philanderers some proper pick-up techniques.
2034 - You Know You're Over Forty When... You think ''Grass'' is something to cut and ''Getting a little action'' means your prune juice is working. A perfect 40th birthday gift.
2042 - Cucumbers Are Better Than Men Because... They don't care if you shave your legs, and they never walk around your place when the shades are up. At last, ladies, revenge for all our male chauvinist books.
2059 - Small Busted Women Have Big Hearts. Finally a book that boasts the benefits of being small busted in our society where bigger is better! A super way to bolster the ego of every slender woman.
2061 - I'd Rather Be 40 Than Pregnant... Or worrying about getting into graduate school, or travelling with young children, or getting no respect at a ritzy store. Great moral support for women reaching the diaperless age.
2064 - The Wedding Night - Facing Nuptual Terrors. For brides and grooms alike: What To Do If He Wants To Take Pictures; What To Do If She Won't Come Out Of The Bathroom; and many more hilariously funny situations newlyweds may encounter.
2065 - Best Mom In The World. The world's best Mom is the only one who can unclog toilets, sort everyone's socks and underwear, and bait fish hooks. A super gift for moms.
2066 - Dad, Best Friend In The World... Knows the value of a Sunday nap and knows enough not to give mom and the kids driving lessons. He is an expert explainer of the facts of life. A perfect gift for every father's day occasion.
2067 - It's Time To Retire When... Your boss is younger than you are, you stop to think and sometimes forget to start again, or you feel like the morning after and you swear you haven't been anywhere.
2068 - Sex Manual For People Over 30. Includes great excuses for non-performance, rediscovering foreplay, and how to tell an orgasm from a heart attack.

2101 - Peter Pecker's Guide To The Male Organ. A detailed analysis of the types of men who own Wee Wees, Members, Weenies, Dinks, Schlongs, No Nos, Tools, Wangs, and many others. Everyone is covered, from accountants to taxi drivers.
2102 - You Know You're Over 50 When... You add ''God willing'' to the end of most of your statements and you don't care where your wife goes when she goes out, as long as you don't have to go with her. A great 50 year old birthday gift.
2109 - The Get Well Book. Cheer up sick folks with this book that teaches them how to gain sympathy, what the doctor really means and how to cope with phones, kids, germs and critters that make you sick.
2121 - More Dirty Crosswords. This latest edition of dirty crosswords will test your analytical powers even further as you struggle to improve your vocabulary.
2123 - You Know You're Over 60 When... You're 60 when you start straddling two road lanes, you start looking forward to dull evenings at home, and you can't remember when prunes and figs weren't a regular part of your diet.
2126 - After All These Years. An Anniversary Book. Gives all the pluses and problems of marriage from learning to sleep without pillows or blanket to having someone around who can find all the really itchy spots on your back.
2127 - Your Golf Game Is In Big Trouble When... Your practice rounds are all in the bar and you've tried out 30 putters and none of them work and you play whole rounds without once hitting the fairway.
2129 - Fun In The John. More fun than you ever dreamed possible. Crosswords, Bathroom Lists, Word Searches, Mystery Games, John Horoscopes, Connect The Dots, Mazes, and Much More.
2130 - How To Tell If It Was Good. It was good if your partner can't stop repeating your name. It was bad if your partner can't remember your name. It was good if your partner wrote you poetry. It was bad if your partner wrote you a prescription.
2131 - The Fart Book. Farts are divided into two groups. 1. Your farts. 2. Somebody else's fart. This book lists them all, the Little Girls Don't Fart Fart, The Dog Did It Fart, the S'cuse me Fart and many more.
2136 - The Shit List. The list is quite extensive and describes the versatile use of this clever word. There is, for example, ''chicken shit'' and ''give a shit'' and ''shoot the shit''. A very funny book, noshit.
2142 - It's Nifty To Be 50. A new birthday book for women. It's Nifty to Be 50 when the kids are old enough to help willingly, and you can't be talked into activities you don't like in weather you hate.

2144 - Women Make Better Bosses Because... They understand when your child is sick, don't look down your dress and they'll hire cute guys for the office.
2149 - Working Mothers Don't Need Vacations and Other Myths. Of course, they have self-cleaning bathrooms, husbands who help and understanding bosses.
2152 - True Love Is... Keeping each other's secrets, sharing desserts and tolerating each other's pets.
2153 - Fart Part II. This sequel covers the dreaded ''Thank God I'm Alone Fart'', the insidious ''SBD Fart'' and the awe-inspiring ''Sonic Boom Fart''.
2156 - Pumping Tush. For all you exercise fanatics. Bridget explains locker room smells and gives suggestions for avoiding gasps in community showers.
2162 - The Booger Book. All boogers can be divided into two groups: 1) dry boogers; 2) wet boogers. This book covers them all, from the swimmer's booger to types of booger disposal techniques.
2165 - The Professional Homemaker Is... A Plumber, a Veterinary Assistant, a TV Analyst, a Domestic Management Specialist & many other things.
2166 - You've Survived Catholic School When... You can enter a phone booth without feeling you should begin confessing and you don't shudder when someone hands you a ruler.
2167 - The Official Chinese Sex Manual. An hour later you're horny again. Covers everything from petting below the pigtail to achieving orgasm with your chopsticks.
2168 - You Know You're A Year Older When... You no longer eat all the dessert just because it's there and you can no longer easily sleep till noon.
2169 - The Curse. Tasteful, sensitive, very funny and sympathetic. It's about a subject that plagues women each month.
2170 - If Your Birthday Falls On A Workday. Everything from how to get the day off to eating ice cream without a spoon.
2171 - Compliments To The Cook. ''Great cooks never serve vegetables people can't spell'' and ''always have plausible excuses and sincere apologies ready.''
2172 - The Perfect Lover. Turns into a pizza at 3 a.m., holds a Ph.D. in back rubbing & gets into bed first on cold nights just so you'll have warm sheets.
2173 - The Burp Book. Includes the difference between a burp and a belch; the skinny kid burp, the silent burp, the complimentary belch and many more.
2174 - Keep Fit With Drink. The Alcorobic way to build a better body. Walking the Line, the Sit-up, the Heave and more.
2175 - Asses. The complete directory of asses of all kinds from the Male Biker's Buns to the Oh Wow! Ass.

2176 - The First Time. From ''how to tell if your date is thinking about sex'' to ''five great excuses for leaving in the middle of the night.''
2177 - You're Over The Hill When... No one cares anymore about what you did in high school, and you see your old cereal bowl in an antique shop.
2178 - The Pregnant Father. The Pregnant Father's chief duty during delivery is to hold a little pan while his wife throws up into it...and much more!
2179 - Irish Sex Manual. Great Irish lovers share their favorite positions. Learn why Irish women are better and what Irish men love about sex.
2180 - Italian Sex Manual. Covers everything from picking up Italian men to great Italian sex games and why Italian men are better lovers.
2181 - Jewish Sex Manual. Includes detailed information about what Jewish women love about sex, how to pick up Jewish men and great Jewish blind dates.
2182 - Life Is Too Short To Date Ugly Men. Life is too short to forgo exotic vacations or never to cheat on your diet!
2183 - 50 Is Fine If You Look 39... And you can eat a hot fudge sundae without worrying about breaking out. Plus many more!
2184 - 60 Is Fine If You Look 39... And you can buy the car you want without worrying over whether it will hold ten kids, musical instruments and dogs. And more!
2186 - 40 Is Fine If You Look 29... And you're still the same old tiger on the road, and they start to trust you at banks and you can still party with the best of them. For MEN.
2187 - Big Busted Women Have More Fun... Big busted women somehow seem more motherly, get the most out of stretch fabric and always know where to look for a lost earring.
2188 - Great Sex For Busy Couples... Explains how to find the time, the place and the desire when two careers keep the couple running.
2189 - You're Aged To Perfection When... You stop worrying about your weight and you're smart enough to save out-of-style clothing until it becomes fashionable again.
2190 - Teddy Bears Are Better Than Men Because... They don't hog the whole bed and they invariably understand when you have a headache.
2191 - Your Skiing's Going Downhill When... Ski shops refuse to tune your skis and you start thinking about the hot tub before your first run.

IVORY TOWER PUBLISHING CO., INC. 125 Walnut Street, Watertown, MA 02172 (617) 923-1111